Part Sun, Part Shade

Part Sun,

Part Shade

Selected poems and photos

Ellie Eich

Cover Design & Typography: Patti Buttitta

ISBN: 978-0-578-22000-0

For Michael

Contents

"So come my friends, be not afraid

We are so lightly here

It is in love that we are made

In love we disappear"

Leonard Cohen

I

Flying among Cloudforms

Everything changes, everything changes.
20-year-olds become 40-somethings;
babies turn into teenagers,
brothers become ashes and return to earth

o my heart, this is not the news of ecstasy.

Karlheinz found another beginning at the
exact crossing point of four wide directions
under an Idaho-looking sky on an icy evening.

Under that same sky in May we walk in honor
of those gone, of those still here. The strange
finality of leave-taking, the abandonment.

The clouds that seem to sit in the vast dome
overhead, that appear dependable in their
strategically perfect placement. And we human

two-leggeds wander around beneath, hearts
full of past, the beginnings and endings of love:
a car accident, an incomprehensible disappearance...

ah, the pathways of a human life.
the winters that do at last give way
to a spring as surprising as it is glorious

happening not as a block of weeks or months
but again and again in a moment of grace after what
appears like eons of an enduring grit.

Snow-melt. One finds one's way back to the living
after the leavetaking. One finds oneself again
(more or less) whole, sailing without a motor

among
   apparently dependable
            cloud formations.

Every morning

Every morning I wake up around 5:15
And wonder what everyone I know is doing
Are they awake too? Do they worry about
how many taxes they'll have to pay
or whether the roof will finally get fixed this year?

It's 5:30 now and I'm in that loop of remembering the ones
who've made me smile
and the moments - blissful, unsought, overflowing -
luminous afternoons in April reading aloud in Spanish
poppies around the pond, rose petals with their Himalayan
temple-scent all in perfect momentary alignment

A horse stands in his hilly pasture, alone. He is not
worrying about taxes or whether he got enough sleep.
He is waiting for me, the one with the carrots and the long
strokes on his muscled neck that turn him into a big horse-
baby who rests his huge head heavy
on my shoulder, mouthing gently

7:20 now, and I've fallen into some kind of trance
Soothed by strokes of memory, reflections, breath
- astonishing steadfast breath that moves in its trajectory
from "outside" to "inside", often neglected by the
indweller but always marvelously, unaccountably reliable

Daylight, and I hear the first shrill squawk of the bluejay
as he flies from lilac to bamboo to the top of the woodshed
awake now, we - in this bright shared sphere

Belonging

In the night
I turn to you once again
it is not so much the you
who is seen with eyes or who
can be touched skin upon skin

it is an inner turning
to a you who cannot really be
known except in this deep
        quiet night way
who in your vastness
receives me in mine
floats into my vacant corners
spreads itself sweetly
in strange otherness
over all my utter strangeness

so that again, we are
who we are
distinct one to the other
and at the same time
like fragrance around orange blossoms
or clouds tinged by setting suns
    belonging
as all things do
  to each other

Birds of a Morning in Winter

Scarlet brilliance has already
become vast transparent gray
ohi'a trees sway,
rub their newly grown tips
on the morning air
doves and cardinals call to each other
with Charlie Parker enthusiasm
and I, another two-legged,
wander outside to sit on the overlook staircase

Thoughts of India,
those raucous dusty chai mornings
smoky-dry air laced with the scent
of onion paratha
small-boned women, straight-backed
with baskets full of stones on their heads
at work on the banks of the nearby canal

Rain here on the leaves
mind meandering,
California to Germany
thirsty, sage-flavored hills
coyote silhouettes on the edge of the great city
damp gray of a south German summer afternoon
ripe raspberries in the forest

Now
this green world
dogs wake up, their companionship
its own sunshine
small intervals of silence
not an absence of sound
but an offering of repose
a field of expanse where all things appear

In the Garden

Today I fell in love again -
this time it was with the light
falling onto creation

Sunbeams overflowed
through the atmosphere
landing on impatiens
leaking over wild orchids
pouring through hibiscus and areca

Today I fell in love with brilliance.
Even the air was infused with
this glow, like skin moist
with oil and sweat

Life from within
echoes profusion
and I drift
through the world
another creature
awash in light

Seeing

Crickets fade to silence
birds open their throats
a slow dawn emerges

sky stained grey
with a faint green
bamboo forest glow

thoughts feelings memories
breath in a wave
washes forward, back

waves the look of water
water the texture of being
color   flavor
swirl   still

now light and eyes to see
mind still ponders the expanse
thoughts the great perfection

body with its strange life
breath the mystery force
"whatever sees"
the ineffable tapestry

For Mary Ann

Two days ago I heard that
Mary Ann had died in a car crash

Today, it strikes home

no more haiku
no more cricketsong
no more looking at Mars in the late August sky
the biggest and brightest he'll be
for another 250 years
no more hearing sirens, dogbarks
coyote-howls or cat-talk
no more cell phone conversations in bookstores
no more annoyance, no more delight
no more paying over 3 dollars a gallon for gas
no more worries over money
or career changes
no more career changes
no more pizza, no more rock n roll
no mountains in mist or oceans in fog
no sunburn, frostbite, spiderbite or bedbug
no father, no mother
no whale-spouting vistas on the deep blue sea
no foot to put in one's mouth
no more slow and methodical
no more sleepless nights, sleepy days
no nail polish, hair dye, lip gloss, sunscreen
no job to be late for, no fear of old age
no more this, no more that

Sweet Pioneer, on to another sphere . . .
May you be safe and well on your journey forth

New Life

This afternoon, earth-scent flying across the yard
through the open window:
Michael digging a new garden bed
The clink of stone against metal
as polaski and muscled arm coax open the stony ground

Inside, I massage a calf, a shoulder
sinewy strands of an upper trapezius
needles, cups, warm stones
soothe, release, flow

I smell the earth as she breathes out
A tiny snore erupts from the man
on the table and
the wind, with its invisible softness
whispers spring's secrets

Tales of grown Toscana Kale
the cardinal couple hidden in the grove
And nearby the wild orchid
its rose-magenta flower
pillaring into the blue

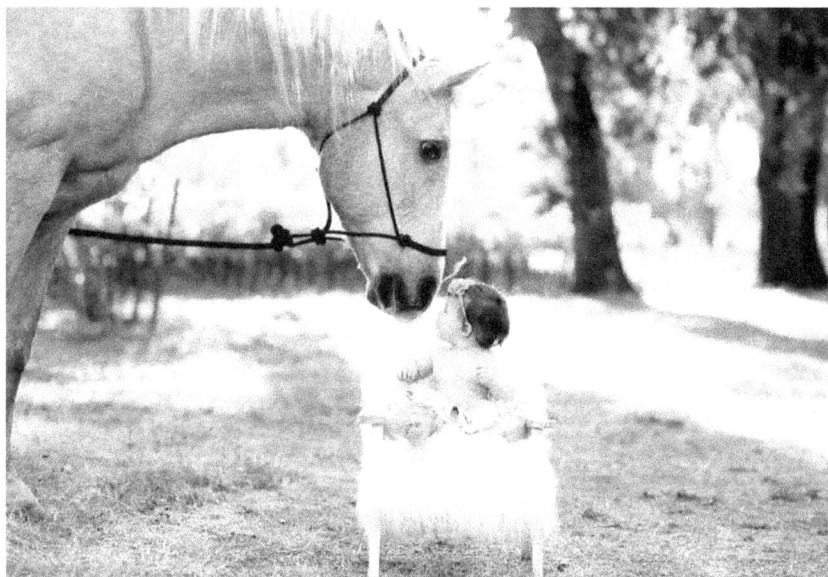

Horse

Just standing next to her
across the rickety fence
her scent a meadow of dried herbs
I am saved from the news of the world

Powerful body, genteel presence
polite, even with her hunger for carrots
delicately she receives them

After there are no more
she licks my hand thoughtfully
snuffles with the wisdom of enough
stands quietly, large, fine head next to mine

She's called Rain, with a dappled coat
and strawberry blond hair
her world the daily search
for the tastiest herbs and grasses

For moments, our heads together
her scent all of me I know
we have disappeared each into the other
horse human
field
sky

Evening song

Three times now as the evening
curtain is dropping
I have heard it:
almost like someone is
plucking a string
and then another silvery note -
an answer? a request?
sounds across the opening
delicate and rare
unlike the raucous enthusiasm
of Puerto Rican tree frogs

These little chirps bring an end to   -
my wild weeding and tumbling thoughts
Slowly my ears become as large
as the leaves of the *wili-wili*
clearer now -
perhaps toad-code for:
daylight wanes,
let's stand under the next downpour

Night drifting

This mind with its multifold versions of unrest
ghosts about in the night
Reaches and probes with inaudible passcodes
casting about for the one weave
to enfold the vague gloom of unease

Let me walk as one, not two.

Leave the window open, that the cautious deer
the rabbits who hide in the tall grass
the fox and coyote and snow-white crane
can all enter to show me the way
through the wildlands of this heart

Parting

After the fire
they returned to their
homelands, and each
was different

A chance encounter
raindrops on the sidewalk
the scent of pines in September
love moments
the color of Alabama

After all was said and done
they returned
 to other lands
to flourish like impatiens
to catch the settling dust
to radiate their own brightness

Another Winter morning

Young dove atop
Chinese Chestnut tree
Listens to the waning moon

Ohias sway in the light
Dove-coo, finch and cardinal
Fill the ears of morning

Old winter heart
Enough of sadness and woe!
Soak up the warming sun

Sky in the mud puddle
Bird-scratch along the roof
Hot chai, may we abide

Pilgrimage

A dream a journey a train station a
large crowd and I find myself,
find myself in another dream
standing at a long wooden bar with two
honkytonk women ordering whiskey, straight up.

The fact that I have never, ever had a whiskey "straight up"
is enough to shoot me out of the dream
into this one, this of tawny fields
and darkness before dawn.

I dream again, and this time I am in a bed
next to him whom I cannot name
he is very close
close as a nutrient
as starlight as home
we are nearly skin to skin
and then I feel his fingertip
curving toward the warm secret sea
that has been dreaming of him

Uncertain perennial crossing
Pilgrimage from self to other
Delicate as budding orchids
Resilient like wild grass

Perspective

There are times in a room
around a table
when many minds
speak in strange tongues
and I am sent to a
faraway mountaintop
wondering
amidst this harvest of expressions
who it is I am

Suddenly there is your face
across the table
finding me in the high winds.
You offer your eyes, a quiet smile
an invisible hand
The music of our long
and lively companionship
scoops up isolation
returns it to dust

Now only stray images
scattered to the ten directions
what remains?
- your embrace
their departure

II

Adornment

It's 4:30 this still-dark morning
the rain has stopped for the moment
I open the window and sniff the air
sweet and pure as almond blossoms.
The light in the window of the house to the north
is a beacon of warmth in an otherwise dark
expanse of bush, tree, coyote, grassland, fox.

700 years ago while Europeans suffered
the Black Plague and the Great Famine
somewhere in the mountains of Tibet
the consummate master Longchenpa sat, years-long.
He looked in every direction (inward)
and finally said:
Everything
is the adornment of basic space
and nothing else.
A marvelous and magical expression,
amazing and superb.

By now the earth appears to have turned so that daylight is
here
the grey crane couple is out foraging
human beings are dreaming the dreams
of marvelous space.
Looking north again
for moments the world can be seen
cloud across empty sky
mountain and river, two-legged and four-legged
winged and wormlike
all churning and rotating
in perfect spontaneity

Spring

Out in the open orchard
atop a long sweeping slope facing west
two dogs sit together
sniffing the fragrance of grasses and spring earth
awake to the evening air

Coyotes tease from the wild southern bush
and the land, the land
she sighs her delicate green breaths
into our old thirsty human-ness.

How does this happen?

Every year I ask this
for the very first time
while my wondering heart, the May bride
builds a temple around the scent
of jasmine on the porch

Tropics

Sunday morning
raindrops hit thick wide
leaves of the breadfruit tree

quiet cloudcover
envelops the land

time chased off by bird
sitting on branch
    dripping,
      singing

There's no moment like this:
the delicate roaring rain
leaves receiving it
mouths wide

its abundance
slides off later
in small avalanches
onto the earth below

World Leaders

I like to think of them sleeping:
all strains and posturings
cast aside, slipping into the dependable
   quiet cavern
where everyone on earth becomes equally
   and unremarkably no one.

I like to picture them
letting out a last involuntary sigh
that might just allow Allah or God
the chance to take over for awhile
as they drift into nothingness.

I like to imagine the breath on their nostrils
the same as it is on mine.
- their eyes rotating slowly into alpha
      and dreams that might visit:
the magnificent rolling of the sea,
of whales surfacing lazily,
of the blue and the green and the brown
children with their curious open laughter,
their power to look upon each other, knowing they are
cousins.

This is my new work:
to imagine them as ordinary human beings
to not falter over this
to see them with the inner eye of kindness
 again and again
 enter the refuge of sleep
helpless, at last, as babies
nurtured by the same great mother

Into the Evening Forest

In search of the clamorous coqui
shrill calls that erode the twilight hush
drip-drip sounds from an earlier cloudburst
bushes, ferns, ohias, guavas
bow their heads to the gathering darkness

Now, moonlight pours itself
through leaf and branch
to drench everything in its dazzle.

Rocky mountain clouds chased by swift winds
 hurdle through
the dark sky
and all around,
boundless silence
into which you float
like a prayer
before it is spoken.

Wind

Up here on Mauna Kea
wind is lord
it commands clouds to drift earthward
kiss the pale green rounded pu'us

it teases the nodding tufted grasses
into a perpetual dance
it is sound and silence
invisible but mighty

it carries the songs of wild birds
the souls of the ancestors
hawks glide and swoop
testing their wingstrength

it is space around form
the cool stillness
in which the mountain rests
like the way we come to know things

Kindling

Dry redwood is the best
It even sings a little as the slim axe slices through
I would watch my father carefully
quiet king of the chopping block
Thin sticks in a random pile
to gather and stack in the woodshed.

I ached to try my hand at this task

Behind us, the scent of redwoods and bay
In front, house and pygmy forest with its
rhododendron, huckleberry and labrador tea
In winter, the creek foamed its way toward the Pacific
Soft-barked redwoods and towering doug firs
dripping softly onto the cushioned forest floor

Now and ever since
to settle a churning mind
I walk out to the woodshed
Current queen of the chopping block

Axe poised, wood sings
my gift to you not only warmth
but also the spice of my sap

Silent Meditation Retreat

the first ten days of a new life
August 1976, Wilbur Hot Springs
golden grassy full-moon hills,
the fragrance of early morning
slow walks, small sips of chai
a glance at the perfect brown fuzz of almonds
sitting heaped in a sparkling cut-glass bowl

the long quiet sighs of finding oneself
the uncut version
raw and hopeful in 100 degree afternoons
sitting upright, fan rotating
intervals of wind like the breath of angels
stubborn achings, shoulder, neck, head
the steady background beat of comment
memory, association, sensation
~ this, now this, ah, this.

the inescapable evidence of *beginning, middle and end*
be it breath, thought, sensation, mood
the signature of all things in time
within this sensate creaturely thing
the human being/self
so alive, and permeated with not-knowing
where from and where to

something else happens after sundown
the raw intelligence of nature

day's heat slowly diminishes
slight breezes steal across the pungent hills
to visit your skin, touch your mind
moon rises to bathe the land in ivory light
scents summon thirsty memories of prairie days

again the inquiring heart
where from and where to
    not to be known
but beneath this noble sky
and within whatever sees
the amber mountain not far off

Hurricane watch

Slanting rain on the glass
   storm lurks out in the big waters
     somewhere south/southeast
      moving westward

If I were that storm I would definitely charge forth
  throw my windy fists into the firmament
    shake the trees, rattle the windows
    tear at those ubiquitous power lines
     rip and roar and rail and squall

  just all play, letting my muscles
    find their origins and insertions
    the strength of this my storm body
    flexing, extending, rotating, stretching
     medial lateral distal proximal
     flashing crashing . . .
     and then
    slowly beginning
    to fade
   over and out
    into

  another Pacific ocean tradewind
  north/northeasterly, more or less
    sedate and reassuring
    cool

. . . we'll see how this goes   *30 Aug. 03*

December morning on the stairs

On this cool 64 degree morning of ebbing December
I want to sit on the porch
here among the sunbeams
float on the breath of this quiet moment
- do I dare get up to make chai?
will it catapult me into the swarm of the trivial?

A larger nourishment is all around
the effortless drip of condensation
onto the lanai from the roof above
a light wind tugging at tree-limbs
dogs shaking themselves awake
to their own renewable resource

* * *

Making chai does pull you into the world,
but what a world this is.
There's hot spicy ginger root, Salsa Dancer Extraordinaire;
the shy nutmeg, subtle and quietly exotic;
cardamom seed, always ready for a good grind.
These three do the dance with simmering hot water
for some ecstatic 10 minutes, then comes the special blend
PG Tips Black Tea via Johnny's Supermarket
on Highway 9 in Boulder Creek
milk from the cows who wander the hills of Waimea
and another 5 minutes of heat and low rumblings, and ---
voila!
- ready to transport you
into the day's early song:
green beans hanging on the tall vines,
playful dog-snuffle,
distant rooster-crow,
the spiky white-tipped dracaena -----
clear, with a slight chance of mauka showers

Small creatures and large

Today in the garden
dogs chew bones
human carries snippers
and tangelos bend branches
suffused with sweet juice

The rubble of a windstorm
scatters its footprints across the land
Doves and cardinals sing of the night's
choppy, sodden rides on waving limbs

Now, today, gentleness prevails
inside and out
The restless heart is quiet
The sky is about as blue as it can get
and Chickory the hound-pit mix
is working a bone that is
rapidly disappearing beneath her powerjaws

Zena the half-pint wildling Shepherd
wanders from place to place
having hidden hers in a dirtpile
Now she looks at me sleepily
grinning a little
as she finds a shady spot
among the impatiens
makes a few turns, settles down

we wild and civilized ones
fragile, but enduring

Outlaw

Just when you think the young renegade shepherd dog
loyal as she is, has been trained . . .
~ you've passed by the ominous-looking pit bull behind
the fence . . .
the sun is shining into the delicate crimson blossoms of the
tall winter grasses . . .
you slide by the open gate where four large German
Shepherd dogs
~ seriously large ~ live . . .
you walk another 50 yards down the dirt road
where the quiet, unsettled parts start
you let her off the leash so she can run ahead freely

But whoa! She's suddenly turned back, full run,
one quick look round - are they watching?
You shout: *Hey! Hey!* She hesitates for just an instant
and then she's off - at an open gallop (if dogs can gallop)
Straight back to the open gate and the four Shepherd dogs
No ears to hear, only a wildfire willfulness that must have
its way

She returns when she's ready, panting happily
looking just slightly sheepish
and walks on

Chickory

Lying on the floor
  spiraling dog
    folds herself
      into human body

human heart swells with love
 who knows what dog-heart feels?

 probably already
 swelling with love

Last Dog-day on Earth

She's lying down now, breathing hard, she
in that grown-older silky black-haired
Labrador/Australian cowdog body
with her boisterous big-heart boldness

In honor of Mara and all related creatures
the four and the two-legged ones
may we all live with grace
may we all die with grace

Now, to Mara gone into the Great Mystery
I salute your spirit
May it be free as it always was

    To your born-in-a-barn manners
    nosing your way in the door
    and never closing it behind you
    I salute your spirit
    May it be peaceful and safe

To your unquenchable enthusiasm for bodies of water
for sticks around bodies of water
for exuberant loudmouth barking
about sticks around bodies of water
for your coyote-like howls some nights
when the moon was full

For your sharp little bark every morning at 7
and the good-morning catapult onto the bed;
for the welcome-home leaps and the quick face kiss
For your sweet companionship, your constancy
that will not be forgotten

On this first morning of your spiraling absence
one more time I salute your spirit
may you be free from danger
may you be peaceful, may you be well

So Much Older Then

Days and nights of the late year
I find my young self seen
 with another's eyes
 an offering to my own
 in tender newness
.
Sleep eludes me as I wander into
the long-forgotten dream of youth
 first-time experience
 exciting, disheartening

Many illusions those days
relentlessly unveiled by what
could only be a healthy skepticism
Still, a life was touched
however unknowingly

Enlivened by essence
to reach out, receive
zinnias opening to sunlight
the visible and the unseen

Music

This hour
overflows with
his absence
yet his presence
has made itself
   at home
somewhere
in this vastness
considered to be
myself

where is he
who inhabits
his own lands
roaming like a
warrior, a shepherd
   a wolf

and yet just as
   delicately
   like mist
   around
Chinese mountains
   appears
   on my
   threshold
   - unaccountable
   symphony

Utah

Desert horizons, sand after sand
drive-by sagebrush and antelope
dry salt lakes once under water
pass by in a wide warm sweep
ribbon of asphalt stretches east northeast
whispering Rockies in white haze
mile marker sixty-two; five hundred to go

the sun now at my window
sensations of heat
radiating in the illusory vastness
fata morganas on the roadway

a toast in the air to the ones
who labored here
depression wages
a mighty thirst

the night sky
vast and perfect

III

Late August

I love to plant for the fall garden
only two specimens today
Red Russian Kale, with its "heirloom" seeds
that appear
like tiny round bits of dark earth
that if you're not careful
get blown away by the slightest hint of a breeze
    and
the mighty Bright Lights Swiss Chard,
unmistakable,
like slightly mutated peppercorns,
some of them bleached blonds
others traditional brunettes.

In a few days they will awaken
from their warm shelter
and begin their long ascent into
the great bright blue air that allows
a perfect arc of expansion
as they surge forth
to meet their destiny

I will try to not marvel too much
having made solemn vows
to protect them
from deer, thirst, sowbugs, earwigs
and devious, sneaky moles.

They, with or without knowing it,
carry the impossible message
the one that lets you float into music
   the song of the seed sirens
lets you fall into wonderment
tumble into grace.

Swallow-code

The swallow sings sweet song to dawn
in trust the death of night she 'waits;
chanting swallow-code from far anon
a sunlit flight toward heaven's gates.

My soul for birth she yearns so black
for patience! and the constant moon
to not forsake her peace, so wracked
to sing instead a swallow-tune

Loon Lake

Loon Lake, still as the clear sky
in early morning
Later, with the rising of the wind
you ruffle your feathery waters

Your invitation remains open
your fresh life-giving joy
beckons to our ancient wish
to dive into blue

Mother of many little streams
your face changes less dramatically
than ours, born of a more tender flesh
that withers and dries

Still, from year to year
great rocks emerge and disappear
jagged or smooth, round like eggs
from a giant granite bird

We lie upon these mammoth jewels
warming human bodies in early morning sun
the slap of the loon family
as they sail along through the still waters

We remember what does not change
and fall again into refreshing sweetness
that has no reason
to return or to remain

For you

Today, for you, I walk along the Navarro
the river that sings the song of life
In it I hear your song
as true as the stones underfoot
some smooth, some jagged
the trail of your life's passage

Poplar leaves stir overhead
in the afternoon breeze
Butterflies play along the riverbed
and the towering trees along the banks ---
your trees, I always think: redwoods,
doug fir, tanoak, madrone - stand
peaceful in the turning light

I sit and see it for you, with you
the "you" who appears to be lying
in a bed in a room, not well
The you whom I'd know
 anywhere and anyway
behind the guise of frailty
bearing this time with a sense of dignity
in spite of all for which there is no help

May the you who abides
be here, rest now in benevolence
among the trees and the water
the sky and the stones and the creatures

Snapshots

Night

Once in a while, when all the words have been chosen,
uttered, smiled over,
when all thoughts and sentiments have been absorbed,
then silence,
The faint murmur of raindrops on the leaves of the lilac
through the open window,
their flat beat on wood deck, the silken song in the rain
gutter.
We "strange, forked creatures" awash in the surging sea.

Morning

Pomegranate streaks paint the dawn sky.
Coyotes, who filled the night with their high-pitched bone-
chilling screams just off the north field
have found their asylums, bedded down for the daylight
hours along the creekbed
The magnetic-blue California jay squawks commentaries
from the live oak.
Thoughts and sentiments, attuned to their nature, awaken
and set forth on a wander.

How do the Spirits Live

I wonder how the spirits live who have known this life and
left it
what they do without morning or eve, without substantial
respite
No river-swims in summer, no wild geese overhead
no breathless promise of things to come
no words, no dance, no song

This life we know is unsurpassed but still and always
passing
The peerless moments rise up and slide
into memory's dim pathways

We reach to taste the boundless, its essence in us sings
admire sunsets, the tiny sand-grain
the drift of clouds dissolving

To know the carve of love, its glorious mending road
the touch that soothes the tumbled heart
the grace of sweet communion

We live in contradiction no thought can penetrate
Only the boundless sky of mind
Only love can illustrate

Outer Hebrides

       you
in the sun of leanness
       linear
  moving light in childgrace
  bounding free in rabbitgrace

       you
  living seductive nonsense
  sailor of the sea of irony
  you mocked the mongoloid moon
  delighted with your cleverness
  then mocking that
  like any true dedicated sailor

       you
  in heavy-lidded nonchalance
       never fooled me
  I only wanted to lie with you
  in a field with a blue ceiling
  feel your arm under my head
  and around my shoulder

and if there is a high tide calm
　　it is you inside me
　　　　very quietly
in sunwarmth and grassbreezes

and if there is remembering
it is me inside me
　　quietly now
in an autumn-yellow oakgrove

　　I feel still your body
　slender and dusky-pale
　acute in simple maleness
　all the sleek lines
　from neck to shoulders to chest
　　　from hips
　　　to belly
　　　to infinity

Sierra Conservation Camp

Into and out of icy late winter fog
within the greening foothills
strange moonscape rocks in silent groupings
    fleshy, smooth,
 others sagittal, aiming skyward
oaks and chemise, cows and sheep
--- primordial harmony,
   hardly a human sign.
    We breathe sighs
like song in the morning

In the camp we all collect
   the loving, the beloved
a large noisy well-lit room
inmates sit at the same observable
   angle at each table
   orange plastic chairs
the visitors cluster haphazardly
 while these men dressed carefully
in their prison blues
    washed combed fed
      find their seats

Some hold their children
others gaze, are gazed upon
        hands
find each other in this small
  controlled world
I like to think that great depths are explored
real tenderness revealed
perhaps for the first time
  I do see faces aglow
the luminous room seems to rock
with a pale orange warmth like the
last moments of a sunset
everything starker, more precious
poised at the edge of transcendence

Another Drunken Boat

moon-luminous man
with your unsculpted street-wise body
your sovereign eyes
eyes that have seen many worlds

I dreamed you were sitting next to me
you were playing some fine jazz guitar
it was tuned in a way
I had never encountered

you were cool as you showed me
your fingers moving along the frets
opening gently my cellar doors
your otherness a spring

where I could slake this searing illogical thirst
and you sang too
your voice dark like the night-sea surge
and I in my boat, pitching among the waves

Wild Grey Geese

wild grey geese in their two million
year old formation
necks out, wing-flaps steady

I wonder what they are hearing
if by now the roar of civilization
is programmed into their genes to sound
like very loud frogs

Threshold

Careful, they said and did not
have to say
shy and halting
as young colts
or the doe who with delicate steps
drifts into a garden to taste
the first leaves of the rose in spring

Untamed too, they meet
each with a quiet hunger
recognized in the eyes of other
known in a flash as self

Cautious as cats in a rainstorm
they sniff out boundary lines
absorbed in unknown terrain

Gradual, astonishing trust
a dwelling reveals itself
multi-storied
 portal

Just this

Just the intermittent calls of birds
piercing the morning forest halls

The translucent pink heads of impatiens
lifting out of their green stemminess
   (also translucent)
   into the cool air

The air: ubiquitous, invisible, spacious
the air that moves the rose-colored cloth
   hanging on the clothesline in sunshine

the four orchids, waiting for their next home
   in the crook of the tangelo tree

the Thai basil, dreaming in still-shade
its place between the sweet white pineapple and
the thorny tang of miniature Kaffir lime leaf tree
living under deep-green fiddlehead fern

The Waiting Man

The waiting man awakens one morning
to the song of the grey dove

Everything had changed
His feet were laughing

His gaze fell into the deep
blue of the ginger blossom

He tucked the mountain
into the fold of his shoulder and

strode into the day that was
to become his life

Opening

Yesterday, in the stillness of late afternoon,
   I set off with clippers and cutters
to discover a tangled brushy corner of woods.
Mosquitoes sang insistently in my ears
the leaves dripped green tickings
and all around, the scent of decay
in its tireless cycle
the moon gaze of eyes beyond time

I wanted nothing more than to disappear
 into that sweet, forgiving neutral Ground.

On the floor of the forest, red upstarts of ginger surged
skyward
  mahogany snarls of dead fern poked stubbornly at ankles
and arms
 and serene in the background, three giant boulder
creatures
silently cultured soft, stubbly vibrant green moss
 on their pocked and crevassed flanks

 It appeared so delicate and fresh I wanted to taste it on my
tongue

I wanted to be the tall impatiens, stretching their luscious
pink and coral mouths toward the holes in the canopy,
   to know their cellulose breath, the come-what-may
fearlessness of being broken or crushed and then beginning
again,
   diving with fierce white root-clumps into just-forming
soil . . .

Then the rain began, softly at first, and birds began their
callings.

I breathed in the dying of the day, stood for awhile
   with the boulders and the shadows
    then took my two new legs
   my tools of benevolent and careful revelation
   and plunged back into the human realm
       its dream of living forever
   .

Part Sun, Part Shade

We wander in a solitary valley
arrive at a door and ask
what is time
that eats away
at all that is
what is this dream of a life
that only ashes and memory remain

The garden offers its own wisdom
the balance of sun, shade, water
seed to shoot to fullness
then gradual - or sudden - withering and decay
and beginnings anew, steady and true

We pour ourselves into the world
 and it beckons:
you - become somebody
 and later, just as playfully,
leave that now.

Human life nothing short
of a presentation unfathomable and grand
Keys unlock long-closed doors
affinities sweep and surge

All of it we are:
streaming fields
devotees crossing pathways
high priests in a great Chinese puzzle
the bewildered blind in a masterful maze

To unveil love's first nature
- that it has no destination –
effortless as a breeze or a baby's smile
ever in renewal
tropics to snowfields
in sunshine and shadow
flowers and thorns equal offerings

Moonlight

How many full moons do we know in a lifetime?

I would like to be entirely versed in each one
remember the hidden corners that each one illumined
and the sublime perfume of the land
written into the night air by oaks and madrones
redwoods and bay laurel
jasmine, butterfly bush and sweet pea
I would like it if that fragrance lived within me as constant
as the moon in its pathway
and as generous in the offering of itself to all

I would like to remember that this is the same moon that
floats across all
skies on this earth, and the fragrance there in the night air
and in you
is its own and also the same. For the earth spins and the
moon returns
and though every thing constantly vanishes from our eyes
and ears and minds
through it all the ancient laws remain, the turning and
returning
to the one who knows in this one moment.

I would like to remember that it's the sun who makes the
moon shine
and what makes the sun shine is nobody's doing and
everyone's
That our time of living on the earth and looking at the sky
is not measurable in years but in how we learn to bear
the yearning that has no end to its bite

That the blaze of longing be its own consummation
the assent for knowing things that can and cannot be
and in that consent the heart's freedom and joy.

Acknowledgements

My thanks to the friends, animals and all creatures who have connected, inspired, nourished and accompanied me along the way.

Heartfelt thanks to Patrick H. Moore, friend and conscientious editor; and to Patti Buttitta, who walked with me through the maze of unknowns. And a special thank you to Lindsay Hildreth for the wonderful photograph of Montana and Young Mira in deep communion.